TRAVEL-TRAILER HOMESTEADING UNDER $5,000

by
Brian D. Kelling

with an Introduction
by
Bill Kaysing

Loompanics Unlimited
Port Townsend, Washington

This book is sold for information purposes only. Neither the author nor the publisher will be held accountable for the use or misuse of the information contained in this book.

Travel-Trailer Homesteading Under $5,000
© 1995 by Brian D. Kelling

Published by:
Loompanics Unlimited
PO Box 1197
Port Townsend, WA 98368
Loompanics Unlimited is a division of Loompanics Enterprises, Inc.

ISBN 1-55950-132-4
Library of Congress Card Catalog 95-77394

Contents

Introduction
by Bill Kaysing

Books don't need to be long and wordy to provide a vital by-product... additional creative ideas of your own! This brief but comprehensive guide to self sufficiency and economic independence generates spin-off ideas on virtually every page. It's a book with a built-in bonus comprised of solid facts inspiring your own imagination. So, as you read it, encourage yourself to visualize all the wonderful variations on the basic theme.

First of all, imagine owning a cozy, compact home on your own paid-for, countryside land for less than a few mortgage payments on a ticky-tacky plaster box in some smoggy city. Now that's a back-to-the-land dream for almost anyone from a young honeymoon couple to a pair of seniors looking for a way to stretch that modest Social Security check. There's no hype in what you are about to read. Everything presented in this real-life narrative is practical, sensible and within the physical capability and financial power of just about anyone of average health and means. The proof is manifest; it's all been done and the photos prove it!

The Land

Start your alternative and complementary ideas flowing with the base requirement... land. Despite its runaway cost in an urban environment, there are millions of acres of remote, desirable country land in all parts of North America.

Often it can be purchased for a few hundred dollars an acre, cash or terms.

In this era of creative financing, you have a choice of many other possibilities. Lease-option is a way to make affordable payments like rent. If the land proves to be to your complete satisfaction after a period of time, you can convert to a regular sales contract.

If you are short of cash, consider claiming the 20 acres of a mining claim. Every American citizen is entitled to this largesse for a reasonable filing fee. The only stipulations of any consequence are those requiring the presence of some mineral deposit of value and the improvement of the claim by a specific value each year. It is legal to bring a trailer onto the claim as long as it pertains to the claim itself, which it certainly would if you planned to live in it while developing the claim. For more information, see the Bureau of Land Management Office in the county or area of your choice.

Another idea of land acquisition is carried out by people who form cooperatives. Five or ten couples will join up, create an informal group, pool their available funds and buy as much acreage as they need to create a "pioneer" village. Coincidentally, it's already being done by owners of mobile homes and recreational vehicles in many parts of the Southwest, especially Arizona and Texas. The team then helps its members put in water and sewer systems and other utilities needed to service whatever movable shelters they wish to use.

Once you start roaming the area of your choice, it is likely that additional ideas will materialize. Keep in mind that sellers are often more anxious to make equitable deals than are buyers. So keep an open mind.

Shelter

Travel trailers are ideal for instant shelter on your newly-acquired land. It's likely that you'll find what fills your needs within a reasonable distance. However, if this doesn't happen, consider some alternatives. Keep an eye open for a motorhome with a blown motor or damaged metal where the cost of repairs exceeds the unit value. This is not uncommon for all kinds of vehicles these days because labor costs for repairs have gone through the roof!

Imagine planting a once-operable but still stylish and handsome motorhome on your wooded acre. Makes sense in many ways including environmental conservation. Putting a want ad in a trailer or motorhome magazine for an inoperable unit would probably bring many responses. Phone nearby auto and truck dismantling yards. They often have damaged recreational vehicles which no one has thought of as a permanently-placed country home. In this case, linear thinking is to your advantage.

Federal, state, county and city governmental bodies often hold auctions of surplus vehicles, and prices can be extremely low. This would be especially true for anything that has to be towed. Check with the departments that would have a use for movable shelter such as mobile labs or offices. The military also disposes of unwanted vehicles at regular intervals. Some types, such as a field command post, would be readily adaptable to home conversion.

So if it has wheels and a roof, put it on your list. You might want to consider what is done in Baja California, Mexico. Very small trailers are added-on.Quite large living rooms are built adjacent to the small basic unit thus giving you all the space you'll need. And if the trailers you acquire are really tiny, simply use two or even three. Visualize three in a U-shape with a patio in the open space.

Water

Scattered across the Western U.S. are thousands of warm and hot springs, many of them totally unused or only partially utilized. Check out a copy of *Great Hot Springs of The*

West from your local library and see if any of the thermal spring locations are compatible with your choice of locale.

Let's say you are one of those lucky people to whom everything good always happens. You are able to buy land with an artesian or free-flowing hot springs of healthful mineral water. Now you are home free. The hot water can be used for your shower, bath, or kitchen. The incoming water can be piped just beneath the floor, giving the room a delightfully warm and cozy quality.

Income? Yes, it's possible to bottle mineral water and sell it. Today there's a large market for anything that's pure and natural. Yes indeed, a thermal spring could make a country homestead a unique paradise.

The University of Arizona Geology Department discovered a way to create a water supply that required no power. They drilled a water well into a mountain side at a slight upward angle so that the water flowed by gravity into a holding tank. So, if your homestead happens to be located near a hill or mountainside, get in touch with the University of Arizona in Tucson and see what the latest slant-drilling techniques are.

In regions of some rainfall, innovative landowners have sometimes built collection basins leading to cisterns. If your land slopes a bit and the annual rainfall is encouraging, you might install a plastic test basin to see what your yield would be. While the water might not be drinking grade, it could suffice for all other uses.

Water is so important to daily life that locating on or near a river, stream or lake might well be worth the increased cost of land for such a location. You and your budget are the key elements for that critical decision.

Power

Praise be to the technologists who have earned our thanks by developing so many alternative energy sources. In addition to the solar-powered, photo-voltaic cells that you'll soon read about, there are myriad methods of creating your own power from such natural sources as wind, water, tides, bio-digesters and on and on.

Old-style windmills still pump water all over the U.S. and will continue to do so for many years to come. If you can buy one secondhand it could be a worthwhile investment, assuming, of course, you have a producing well.

There are lots of homemade direct-current generators producing storable current. Check for plans in such magazines as *Mother Earth News*, available at most newsstands.

If you located near a steady flow of water, consider a small hydroelectric generating plant. These are often homemade wooden water wheels driving a recycled auto alternator. Plans can be found in country magazines and those dealing with popular science applications.

Summary and Conclusions

Details on the septic system, heat and refrigeration are so specific they hardly warrant any additional comments. Follow these and the other instructions and you're more likely to end up with a paid-up homestead yielding unlimited joy, potential and freedom.

Just think of all the time you will have to yourself! No more highway commutes, traffic jams, or any of the other urban blues that stole your very life away. Then there's the grand opportunity to fulfill your potential as a person.

One must conclude that by owning a mortgage- and rent-free home in the country many exciting lifestyle options become viable.

With a PC or a phone you can plug yourself into the wide world of high-tech information in order to learn as much as you wish. You only need a PO box to tap the literary resources for both buying and selling. Have lots of room? Consider growing specialty items such as gourmet produce and exotic medicinal and gourmet herbs, as well as raising rare birds and animals.

Time, space and freedom from economic stresses will grant you the best things in life...

- Boundless health
- Effortless autonomy
- Relaxation anytime
- Self-sufficient security for you and your family
- Capability to choose your associates
- No limits to exercising your creativity
- Being close to nature and the spiritual world

Obviously, this inexpensive way of life will become more popular as more and more people prove its inherent success by achieving their chosen goals. Start now when you can take your choice of locations, and be the first one on your block to become the king or queen of your own mountain!

"The ideal day never comes. Today is ideal for anyone who makes it so."

H.W. Dresser

Preface

The object of this book is to show you how to purchase and set up a complete RV homestead for under $5,000, land and trailer included.

You'll have all the comforts of home: power, heat, pressurized water, refrigeration and a septic system.

Sound too good to be true? It's not — I did it, and I'll show you how.

I live in a 21-foot travel trailer on 5 acres in southern Colorado. Everything is paid for, and I have all I need in creature comforts.

There are only four prerequisites: the money, a pickup truck, tools and the willingness. But before you sell everything and start off, I suggest you read this entire manual thoroughly.

Chapter 1
Cost Breakdown

The following figures are based on my situation:

Land	2,195
Trailer	1,200
Skirting	75
Generator	200
Heat	105
(Woodstove 80)	
(Flue/accs. 25)	
Propane tank	241
Solar power	625
(Solar Panels 215)	
(Batteries 260)	
(Platform 70)	
(Power Inverter 80)	
Septic System	70
Cistern	49
(Pump 19)	
(Barrels 15)	
(Pipe 5)	
Air pump	5
TV antenna	23
Mailbox	7

TOTAL	**$4,795**

Chapter 2
Tools You'll Need

Chain saw
Circular saw
Jigsaw
Handsaw
Hacksaw
Drill and bits
Phillips bits for drill
Screwdrivers
Tape measure
Level
Power cord
Caulking gun
Wood rasp
Tin snips
Shovel
The usual assortment of automotive tools.

Chapter 3
The Land

Figure 1
The land

Choosing your land is probably your most important consideration, and there are many things to take into account.

For starters, where would you *like* to live? To me, this is the most important question.

Then, where can you *afford* to live? Where can you find a piece of suitable land for $2,500 or less?

Is the county zoned? Are mobile homes allowed?

What are the taxes? How far is it to town?

Does the county maintain the road? (Assuming there is a road.)

Can you get in in winter? Do you have a four-wheel drive? (Strongly recommended.)

What's the climate like? Is there a lot of sun?

How far to water? How far to firewood?

Is the ground suitable for a septic system?

What will you do after the homestead is in? Will you work?

I would start with the question, "Where do you want to live?" Regionally. Say, the West, or the South. From there, narrow it down to a particular state.

In my instance, I knew exactly where I wanted to live: in the San Luis Valley of southern Colorado. I had already purchased a 5-acre tract in Alamosa County a few years back for a total of $2195. I paid $295 down and made monthly payments of $50 until it was paid off. I preferred to have the land — and everything else, for that matter — paid for, but you can sure make payments if you want to. It would substantially drop your initial amount needed to get started from the $5,000 we are talking about in this book. But you have to be able to make the payments.

My taxes are $52 a year, and there is a building inspector to deal with, but I found him most reasonable. For instance, mobile homes are allowed in Alamosa County, but travel trailers are not. However, my trailer is one of many. There are even a few buses. One guy I know built his entire house — complete with artesian well — without a single permit. There's even a straw-bale house down the road a few miles.

Building inspectors are powerful people in big cities, but that's not the case in small towns. I did eventually obtain a building permit, to build a rock house, and this got him off my back. Also, by that time, I had my septic system installed, and that pacified him further.

Anyhow, I love the West, and particularly this part of Colorado. It's sunny almost every day, the views are fantastic, people are friendly and land is cheap.

The San Luis Valley is the largest mountain valley in the world, roughly the size of Massachusetts. The Rocky Mountains run all the way around this valley, and the elevation here at the floor is quite high, 7,550′.

There are still some places available for $2,500, especially in Costilla County, where land is cheaper. Last year, I bought a 5-acre piece there for $1,200, and sold it for $1,500. Costilla County, incidentally, has the added advantage of no zoning, and doesn't even have a building inspector. Taxes there are less than $28 a year on a 5-acre tract. It's a favorite for homesteading. Many people live in trailers or buses, and even have outhouses (why, I can't understand, when for the same cost of materials you can have a septic system — covered later in this book).

There are several artesian wells in this area that are accessible to the public. One is on Highway 160, halfway to Alamosa, and an other in Blanca, in Costilla County. In addition, there are various others scattered here and there throughout the valley. These flow year-round, with good clean water, due to a large aquifer under a layer of clay beneath the valley floor. Actually, there are 2 aquifers — one under the clay, one over. And the clay can be shallow or deep, from 10 feet to over 400, depending on the location.

Under pressure from water flowing underground from the mountains, a puncture of the clay layer (by a well) relieves pressure and yields a constant flow of water to the surface. But you can't get artesian everywhere in the valley. For instance, at my place I can't, because the clay layer is absent this close to the mountains, but I simply wanted to explain how the water flows constantly.

And you need a constant availability of water. The San Luis Valley only gets just over 7″ of precipitation a year, so water collection is not feasible. Trying to drain a roof or other area for water might be fine in places that get a lot of rain, but here, that would bring on thirst in a hurry.

It is quite cold here in the winter, but everybody heats with wood. I just stoke the wood stove and forget about it.

Here is the climatic data:

The San Luis Valley is called the Land of Cool Sunshine. It shines about 320 days a year. So, besides being excellent for solar power, I love it.

It rarely gets into the 90's, with 96 being the highest temperature ever recorded in the valley. We hit 93 last summer, and you should have heard the people complain.

We average 50 nights a year in which the temperature gets below zero. Last winter I counted 35. Minus 10 is nothing. In the last two winters, I have seen it get to -26, once. The coldest temperature ever recorded was an even -50. However, don't let the cold scare you. When the sun comes up in the morning, it quickly warms things. That doesn't mean it will be 60, but it warms up.

With a dry climate like we have, it also seems warmer than it is. There's none of that mushy wet cold like they have in Buffalo, N.Y.

At any rate, no matter where you locate, choose your land with care. You'll spend half your money on this purchase, and it can affect your happiness and economic situation for the future. Don't rush into anything, there's lots out there. On the other hand, don't pass up a perfect deal, either. Trust yourself; you'll know it when you see it.

Chapter 4
Shelter

A travel trailer is the best, because they're cheap, give all the comforts of home, and are easily transportable by ordinary vehicle. Mobile homes give much more room, but also require a greater initial expenditure, usually require a semi-tractor to move, and require more work to set up and maintain.

For this reason, I bought a 21-foot travel trailer in good condition for $1,200. It's a 1972 Concord Traveler, with 15-inch tires, dual axles and electric brakes, which I used. An older trailer of this size weighs approximately 4,200 pounds, and has a tongue (hitch) weight of about 425 pounds.

Naturally, since you will be living in it, the bigger the better, but don't out-do your towing vehicle. I pulled mine with an '84 Grand Wagoneer that had a 360 V8 in it, and it was inadequate, except for engine size. I subsequently had to replace the transfer case in a small town — Cha-ching! I recommend a pickup truck, preferably a ¾-ton. You'll need one anyway.

Besides obvious things like a bunk, you'll need the following items in your trailer:

Kitchen — Sink, stove, propane refrigerator.

Bathroom — Shower, vanity, toilet with holding tank.

Water system — with storage tank and hot water heater.

Propane heater or furnace (for when you're away.)

A 12-volt lighting system (most also have 110 lights.)

Most trailers of this size have this stuff. If the one you're looking at doesn't, I wouldn't buy it, unless it's only lacking the lights. You can easily install a 12-volt lighting system, and in fact, 12-volt fluorescent lights are about 4 times as efficient as 12-volt incandescent bulbs. Or, you may choose to use only a kerosene lamp in the evenings. (Don't use lamp oil, it costs much more, and I don't think it puts out as much light as kerosene.)

When you look at the trailer, make sure it's big enough and comfortable — you'll be spending a lot of time in it. Think about the floor plan. Where will you put the wood stove? I took out half of one couch and installed mine next to the hot water heater.

My trailer also had an apartment-sized electric refrigerator in it when I bought it — a great asset, the owner thought. Wrong. Initially, since I took the third couch out and built a desk for writing, I built in an icebox on one end of the desk, near the door. That's OK, but it needs ice to operate — from town, nearly every day (except in winter, when you can make your own). But still, you have no freezer, and a small RV refrigerator actually costs less to operate than the cost of ice. (This is covered more fully in the refrigeration chapter.)

Everything in the trailer must work, or be fixable. If the propane fridge doesn't, chances are you can fix it. (See the refrigeration chapter.) Dump some water into the holding tank to make sure it doesn't leak. Light all gas appliances. Check the furnace for fumes.

Setting Up

You'll want to situate your trailer in the best possible location on your land, taking advantage of access, sunlight, prevailing wind direction and the view.

When you have that figured out, lay a couple of planks down in front of the tires (make sure they're level) and pull the trailer up onto them. This keeps the tires out of direct contact with the ground — which causes dry-rot — and also gives you a stable starting point.

Then set your trailer solidly on blocks, stands, or sections of logs. Whatever you use, be sure to put a flat piece of wood under the bases. I used the adjustable stands that came with my trailer, and put larger squares of plywood under them.

Use a level on various parts of the trailer while you're tightening up the jacks or stands. Be sure and check the inside floor of the trailer, especially. You can just about get it all from that.

You may want to consider tie-downs for the trailer, if you live in a windy area.

Skirting

Figure 2

Skirting helps a lot. It keeps varmints and bugs out, allows you weather-proof storage under the trailer, keeps the trailer *much* warmer (especially the floor), and helps keep the plumbing and holding tank from freezing. It also looks good, and adds a sense of permanence to it all.

You can probably use a variety of things for skirting, but I recommend barn metal. I have seen fiberglass panels, wood, plywood, and even straw bales used. However, these all have drawbacks. Just look at any old carport or porch with fiberglass panels — they're all broken or cracked. Wood's not so bad, but is a lot of work to install, and requires painting. Plywood sponges water and moisture up from the ground, delaminating in a short time. Straw bales? Mice and bugs.

Galvanized barn metal is the best bet. It's tough, light, easy to install, never needs paint and won't soak up moisture. It comes in convenient sizes, like 2 feet or over in width, and 8-foot lengths.

Figure up the footage you'll need with a measuring tape, allowing for several inches overlap at each joint, including the corners. My trailer needed 9 pieces — 1 for each end and 3 for each side. The extra one comes in handy for the wheel wells, where they arch up.

You'll also need several pounds of self-tapping sheet metal screws, a pound or so of drywall screws, several tubes of caulk, and a few 1 x 4's, which, initially, you'll have laying around.

Before you start, find the best location for access panels. You'll need at least one of these, and preferably two. This panel will lap over and screw onto a regular skirting panel on each end.

Figure how deep your skirting will go into the ground, and dig that narrow trench all the way around the trailer. Now start installing the barn metal, working from a corner.

You will need to run both ends of both sides of the skirting slightly past the ends of the trailer, to make the corners.

You want to lap up the trailer, at least to the trim at the bottom. Make sure the edge of the sheet lies against the trailer, making a nice seal. That is, the wave of the corrugation should curve into the trailer. I lapped up 2 corrugations on the trailer and screwed directly into the plastic trim.

At the ends of the panels, cut a piece of 1 x 4 and attach it behind where the joint will be. Obviously, you can't lap the trailer with this, so cut it short enough to fit underneath — it doesn't have to attach to the RV.

Starting at the end of one side of the trailer, screw the first panel onto the trim, making sure to run past where the corner will be. Then, using drywall screws, attach the 1 x 4 to the sheet. You may want to "back up" the piece of wood to make it easier to screw. If you use your hand, make sure it's out of the way of where the screw will come through. Running a screw into your hand is quite painful, I can assure you. Holding another board or a large hammer behind it works even better.

Now, backfill the trench with dirt behind the first sheet.

Screw the next panel in place, using one self-tapper at the joint. Line up the other end of the second sheet for height, and screw the panel to the trim. Put the remaining screws into the joint (they'll run through the first sheet and into the 1 x 4). Backfill with dirt.

At this point, you're probably up to where your access panel will be. Skipping that space, cut a sheet to complete the run, bearing in mind the distance to go past the corner *and* to lap under the access panel. Install this sheet. Backfill behind it.

Cut your access panel to size and install it with the self-tappers.

Also shear and install a piece to cover the wheel wells, lapping the trim and the panel below it. There's not much you can do about the exposed spaces behind the corrugations on the ends of this little panel except caulk them.

One side is now complete.

Do the other side in the same manner.

For the ends, you'll cut one sheet to fit between both sides. This means you'll cut the waves of the corrugations on both ends of this panel. After measuring for the sheet, do this with the panel lying down, by standing a cut-off piece on edge, directly on the sheet where the corner will be. Trace the general outline of the corrugations with a magic marker, and cut them with tin snips. You don't have to be perfect, you'll caulk this joint anyhow. If you don't want to follow the curve exactly — and you don't need to — you can simply cut the corrugations out in small triangles.

On the front of the trailer, you'll probably have to cut around the frame, gas line, and maybe some wiring. Draw your cutouts or holes with the magic marker, then simply cut down to the center of each from the top of the sheet, and make your cutouts. This leaves as much of the sheet in place as possible, yet still allows for fairly easy installation — you pull out one side of the metal at the cut and slide the sheet up around the obstruction.

Install a 1 x 4 at the corners, onto the end panel of the skirting along the sides of the trailer. Maneuver the sheet into place — this one is perhaps the most difficult — and screw through the panel into the edge of the 1 x 4.

Do the same thing with the rear panel on the trailer. There probably won't be cutouts of any kind. However, the other consideration here is the bumper. Depending on your trailer, you may want to cut around and install it under the bumper, directly to the trailer. On mine, the bumper is a square tube projecting out from the trailer, and I used it as a surface to screw to, bending the sheet over the top of the bumper and securing it with self-tappers. Depending on the thickness of the metal, you may have to drill a hole in the bumper first, just slightly smaller than the self-tapper. Otherwise, you'll snap a bunch of screws off.

Use the 1 x 4 or 2 x 4 in the corners, under the bumper. Screw the panel into place.

Now, caulk the corner joints, all the gaps that need it, and any projections coming through the skirting, such as the frame on the front. Don't caulk the access panels.

The metal fit so well against my trailer that I didn't need to caulk it where the horizontal top line of the skirting curves into the trailer siding. But if you need to, do it.

Also, cut a small access panel — just big enough to get your hand through — where the holding tank valve is. Put a piece over this and screw it on.

Fill dirt against the skirting and you're in business. Isn't it nice to have a warm floor?

Chapter 5
The Septic System

You can build an inexpensive, fully functional septic system for under $100, if you can get the rock free, or at least cheap.

My system cost me a total of $70, with the PVC piping being the greatest portion of the cost.

This is a very simple system, but requires the most output of physical labor to install, if you dig it by hand. I dug mine with a shovel, and I spent over a week alone on the excavation. If you have any neighbors, and one of them should happen to have a backhoe, lucky you.

Since your trailer's plumbing is set up the same as in a regular house, you do not need to install any vents in the septic system itself. If you look on the top of the trailer, you will see at least one plumbing vent sticking up, and more likely two. Your septic system will vent directly through these, as will your holding tank.

You should sink your system deep enough to prevent it from freezing. I have 32 inches of dirt over the tops of my barrels, and the lines are just slightly lower than that.

This system works with 2 barrels, one for solids, and one for liquids. The solids drop into the first barrel, where they are decomposed. The liquids flow into the second barrel, and out the leach line.

For the tanks themselves, you will need 2 plastic barrels, 55-gallon size. I purchased mine from a local honey farm which imports raisin juice concentrate in them. The walls are ¼-inch thick. Mine are blue in color, but I have also seen them in black and white. These are standard-sized drums, with the usual 2 openings in the top. Lids are needed for the openings, as these will be sealed.

Figure 3
Plastic barrel for septic system.

They were $5 each, and simply needed to be washed out. Although it's going to contain sewage, I washed mine out anyway. I want those bacteria down there eating waste, not making fruit salad.

DO NOT use metal barrels, as these will quickly rust out and leak. Your system will be destroyed, and you'll be digging up a dirty mess to install plastic barrels.

For the sewer line itself, from the trailer to the tanks, standard 4-inch PVC plastic plumbing sewer line is used. PVC comes in several grades, but ask for the thin-walled stuff, as the thick-walled is more expensive, and is not required. (But, if it will be inspected, check first for pipe-type requirements.) This comes in 10-foot sections, and one end is flared to accept the regular end of the next section of pipe. Be sure to buy PVC cement to glue the joints together. Chances are, the store owner will also try to sell you primer, which is applied before the glue, but this is unnecessary, and most plumbers don't bother with it.

From the tanks outward, you need a leach-line, also of 4-inch PVC pipe, but perforated just for this purpose. This pipe is available with the holes already drilled, but if they happen to be out of stock, simply buy the solid pipe and drill the holes yourself. It costs about the same for both pipes, so try to buy the pre-drilled kind. The holes are generally about ½-inch in diameter, spaced every 12 inches or so, and are drilled so as to be on both sides of the lower ⅓ of the pipe when installed.

Figure 4
Leach line for septic system.

You will need two 90-degree elbows. You also need a 3-inch to 4-inch adapter fitting, and 2 caps.

The drums are joined together about 4-5 inches up from the bottom with a section of solid 4-inch pipe, about a foot long. (See Figures 5 and 6.) Using the *inside* diameter of a small section of pipe (cut a 2-inch piece off one of the longer sections if you don't have a short piece lying around), trace the circle onto the barrel with a pencil or pen. Be sure it's a round circle — don't crush the pipe with your hands as you trace it, or you'll have an ellipse instead of a circle, and it may leak.

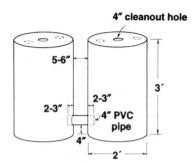

Figure 5
Joining septic barrels.

Drill a hole with a large standard drill bit or paddle bit near the edge of the inside of your circle. The hole needs to be large enough to accommodate the blade of your jig saw. Cut your holes out, being careful to stay either inside of or right on your traced lines. A jigsaw is best turned in a circle by pivoting the saw on the blade; that is, by turning the rear of the saw, not by trying to move the blade over with the pressure of your hand.

After the cut is finished, remove the cut-outs from the barrels, if they fell in, as they could cover or plug one of the lines. Now trim up the cuts with your wood rasp, being careful not to take too much out.

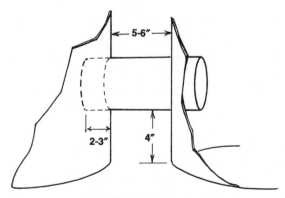

Figure 6
Joining septic barrels.

Take your 1-foot section of 4-inch pipe and try to shove it forcefully into the hole of one of the barrels. It probably won't go at first try, and you'll need to continue filing and trying until you can force the pipe in. You want a tight fit, so as not to leak. The pipe will slide in easier when you caulk the holes, which will provide lubrication.

When you can do this with both barrels, silicone the edges of one of the holes. Also apply silicone to one end of your 1-foot section of pipe, about 3 inches from the end. Run 2 good-sized continuous beads of caulk around the pipe, about ¼-inch apart. Now, laying the barrel on its side, push the pipe into the hole until you make contact with the second bead of silicone. Then leave it.

Caulk the hole in the second barrel, and also the other end of the pipe sticking out of the first barrel. This connection will be harder to make, and when I did it, it was accompanied by some mild cussing. The problem is, you don't have much room to work in between the two barrels. You must grip the connecting pipe itself to shove it into the second barrel; you cannot simply line it up and shove on the first barrel. That would only push the pipe farther into the first drum. So, I would recommend placing the second barrel against something solid, in an upright position, and working the pipe into it with your hands. Again, push it in until you make contact with the second bead of silicone.

The pipe should penetrate into each barrel by several inches. Look down through the openings in the tops to make sure this is so. It doesn't have to be perfect, and if it sticks into one barrel farther than the other, don't worry about it. You should end up with about 5 inches or so between the barrels now.

At this point, find the center of the tops of the barrels, and trace the *outside* of the 2-inch section of pipe you used to trace the 1-foot connection with onto the tops of the barrels. These will be the clean-outs.

Cut these out, being careful again to retrieve the cutouts. I find it easier to drill a second hole directly in the center of the circle, and stick a finger in this hole when you are finishing your cut. This keeps it from dropping into the barrel. Should it fall in anyhow, simply pound a nail into the end of a stick and bend it over like a hook. Use this to fish it out. Now tape over these holes with duct tape.

Next, silicone the existing threaded holes in the tops of the barrels, and install these caps, tight. Go over the edges with silicone, if it hasn't squeezed out, for a good seal.

Now put a lot of silicone around the connecting pipe at the bottom of the barrels, for an extra-good seal. This is perhaps the most important connection in the system.

You are now ready to place the barrels in the hole. Since they are so light, just grab them by the edges of the tops and lower them into the hole. While moving them, try to be careful not to twist or move the barrels around in relation to each other — you want that good seal.

Position the barrels in the center of your hole, as level as the eye allows, and fill in around them with a little dirt, maybe up a foot or so, so the barrels will not move. Don't compact the fill at this point — this will allow for the barrels to expand when they fill with waste.

Now, recheck the depth of your trenches for the sewer line to the trailer and the leach line. EVERYTHING now should work from the height of your barrels. Should you find that your trenches are not deep enough, DO NOT attempt to raise the barrels and allow dirt to fill in underneath. If you do this, they will settle later, possibly crushing the lines in and out, giving you a big headache, and probably another backache when you have to dig up and fix everything. Work from the setting of the barrels, by either filling in or digging more out of your trenches. If you should need to fill your sewer line trench from the trailer, be sure to compact it by walking over the fill until it's hard-packed. (If you have access to water, it's even better to compact the soil around your tank and lines by pouring water over the soil.) The slope of the sewer line must be maintained.

The next step is to install the solid sewer line to your trailer.

Cut another hole in your first (the solids) barrel, the one closest to your trailer. Make this cut up as high as you can on the side of the barrel, just under where the barrel rounds over into the top. You will be following the same procedure with this hole as you did with the 1-foot connecting pipe between the barrels. That is, trace the inside, file, silicone, and shove it in several inches.

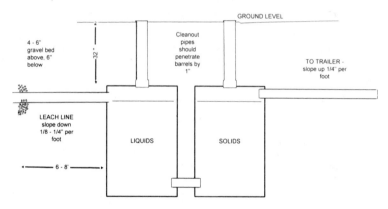

Figure 7
Septic System.

MAKE SURE this line slopes ¼-inch to the foot, UPHILL to the trailer. This is very important. Less than ¼-inch doesn't allow the solids to slide downhill. More than ¼-inch generally allows the liquids to out-pace the solids, and then the solids get stuck on the bottom of the pipe, clogging the sewer line.

Use a level on this. An easy trick to make sure you're getting the right slope is to tape a block of wood of the appropriate thickness on one end of your level. If you're using a 4-foot level, a 1-inch block would be correct (¼-inch to the foot). A 2-foot level would require a ½-inch block.

You can now place the level directly on top of the sewer pipe, and when it reads level, you're right on target.

You want as straight a line from the tank to the trailer as possible, with as few elbows as needed. Ideally, there will be only 2; one at the trailer connection to send the waste downward, and the other directly beneath it, underground, to direct the waste towards the tank.

Figure 8
Septic system.

You may want to install a clean-out in your sewer line, where the line plunges directly downward after turning down from the trailer, just in case you ever need to snake it.

Most trailers use a 3-inch PVC waste pipe, and since we are working with 4-inch pipe, this is where the 3- to 4-inch adapter fitting comes in. The trailer's waste pipe usually has 2 prongs on it to facilitate the connection of the flexible RV sewer pipe. Make sure your adapter will fit the trailer plumbing, and then simply saw the prongs off with a hacksaw. File smooth, and make your connection.

A special consideration here is the trailer's holding tank. Usually, the holding tank holds only toilet waste, and the sinks and shower lines connect to the waste pipe *after* the holding tank valve, allowing them to flow freely at all times.

I recommend leaving the system intact, since not only is it much easier than cutting through the bottom of the trailer and holding tank and trying to rig a connection to the toilet, but also because RV toilets don't send much water down the tubes when they flush, relying instead on the liquid waste that accumulates in the holding tank to flush the solids when the valve is pulled.

I think putting toilet waste directly into the sewer line without a water medium to send the solids on their way will clog your sewer line *muy pronto*.

Also, since the toilet uses so little water, it's usually not sufficient to send the solids to the other end of the holding tank, where the outlet is. RV toilets usually just drop the bowl's contents straight down into the holding tank.

For this reason, I recommend leaving the system intact and using the holding tank. Every other day or so, simply pull the valve and send the sewage on its way. This will necessitate a small access panel in the trailer skirting, to reach the valve. Once a week, after emptying the tank, I send 3 or 4 gallons of water from a jug down the toilet, all at once and in a hurry, to make sure everything reaches the septic system and the lines stay clear.

However, in extremely cold weather, you may want to leave the valve open, so your pipe doesn't freeze solid and burst. In that case, you may want to send a gallon or two down the toilet at the end of the day. But the trailer skirting does wonders in keeping the plumbing warm. I only leave my valve open when the night time temperature will be around zero or below.

The Leach Line

Figure 9
Installing the leach line for the septic system.

From your liquids barrel, you need a leach line leading outward, to carry the liquids away to where they'll be absorbed into the ground.

You should make your hole in this drum several inches lower than the inlet hole (the sewer line from the trailer) in the solids barrel. This will allow the sewage to fall into the septic tank, keeping the level of the tanks lower than the inlet line, so that nothing settles in the sewer line, creating a clog or blockage. I made mine 2½ inches lower. You should make this connection in the same way as the others — trace, cut, file, caulk and shove it in.

The perforated line should start about 8 feet out from the tanks, so the first section of pipe should be solid. You don't want the liquids to seep around the tanks, possibly settling them and destroying the integrity of your system.

The leach line also needs to be sloped, and I used the same ¼-inch to the foot here. It can, however, be slightly less than that, but ⅛-inch per foot is the minimum. To be safe, go ¼-inch.

You only need one line out, as opposed to the multiple lines popularly in use in larger home systems. It should be a straight line — no elbows are required.

The length of your line can vary, depending on your soil conditions and the wetness of the area you live in. In my area, we get just over 7 inches of precipitation a year, and the soil is dry and sandy. My line is 35 feet of perforated pipe, and 8 feet of solid. If you get a lot of rain, I'd suggest making your line a little longer.

Your excavation (ditch) should be about 2 feet wide, and approximately 6 inches deeper than where the pipe will actually be laid, to allow for rock under it. You will need to slope the ditch, along with the pipe. At the end of your trench, dig it wider and deeper, making a pit you can fill with gravel.

The rock should be 1 to 1½ inches in size, and you will need about 3 pickup loads of it. I used red volcanic rock — real light stuff — and got it free from a local aggregate company, which didn't even sell it anymore. There were some piles lying around, and upon asking — *and* spending a few extra minutes talking with the man in charge — they gave it to me for free. They even put one load in my truck with a front-end loader. It also pays to be friendly. Also to live near a small town.

Fill the ditch by eye to the approximate level of the bottom of the pipe. Then start your installation, using the level. The gravel is easy to work with, and can be scraped or kicked around as needed for the proper slope. The perforations, of course, are to be installed towards the bottom of the ditch. I also drilled some ¼-inch holes along the bottom of my pipes, spaced 2 feet apart on the first section, 16 inches on the next, and 1 foot on the third piece. On my last 5-foot section, at the pit, I drilled holes every few inches.

Figure 10
End of the leach line for the septic system.

There are to be *no holes* in the top of the pipes, as this would allow sand and dirt into the pipes, plugging them.

At the end of your leach line, insert a coffee can directly into the end of the pipe and run a few screws through it to seal the line. You're only keeping gravel out, so it isn't necessary to make a water-tight seal.

When the entire line is in place, go ahead and fill the ditch with gravel, covering the top with 6 inches if you can.

Then, cover the gravel with plastic or building paper. This is important, because if you don't cover the gravel, dirt and sand will settle down through it, and — you guessed it — clog the line. That would be a catastrophe, and you'd be digging again. I used 2 layers of clear plastic, the kind you put over windows in the winter. It costs about $2.50.

When this is done, backfill the trench completely.

Next, you want to install clean-outs in the tops of the barrels, where you already have the holes cut and duct-taped. These will be solid 4-inch PVC pipes, running straight up to ground level.

These will need to be self-supporting, and so you must use either a straight connection or the flared end of a pipe. In both cases, you'll need to cut two pieces several inches long, and insert them in the flared ends or connections. This extra width, or "collar," is what holds the pipes up.

Silicone the connections, and brace the pipes in place by wiring or taping them to sticks jammed sideways against the sides of the excavation. Don't spare the caulking here, as the tops of the barrels are bound to sag a little under the weight of the soil above, and you don't want your tanks filling with dirt.

At ground level, slip the PVC caps over the pipes, without caulk.

Now, finish your backfill of the entire excavation.

Congratulations! You are now in business.

I recommend backfilling the tanks as the barrels fill, so they are completely expanded when you fill in the dirt. I didn't compact any of the fill around my tanks, to allow for this. (This is OK in the summer, but make sure you backfill before winter sets in.)

I also recommend inserting bacteria into the tanks to get the system functioning. To start with, I put some down the clean-out of the solids tank. However, you can also simply flush this product down the toilet, or put it in your sink drain. Generally, a septic system promotes its own bacteria, but since this is a small system, I recommend adding it at regular intervals.

A product such as RID-X will do the job, and costs less than $5 a box at a department store. A small box should last you for many months. I add it about every 10 days, about 2 tablespoons at a time.

A system like this takes about 2 weeks to install, but beats an outhouse any day. Especially the cold ones.

Happy flushing.

Chapter 6
Water

You will need a year-round, non-freezing, clean and free supply of water, and it must be close, or at least on your way to town. If you can afford a well, that is the most desirable way to go, of course.

However, assuming you can't (I among you), you will need to haul water to your homestead, unless you happen to have a stream running through your property. Land with streams, however, is non-existent in the price range we are targeting. Should you be able to get such a piece, count your blessings, as you are one of the chosen few.

Barring this, prepare to haul water.

It's not that much of a bother, and since you will have a small storage system (I'm going into that), you will probably only have to do this once every week or two, depending on how well you conserve water.

Water conservation is necessary, but I don't find it restrictive. No, I don't wash my truck here at home, and I do laundry once a week in town (I'm there anyway for groceries and other things), but I still take a shower, flush my toilet at every use, and do dishes every day.

The Trailer

A trailer suitable for our purposes already has a water system in place — this is essential.

It must have a bathroom with toilet, sink, and shower, and also a kitchen sink. It also must have an existing water tank inside the structure, since we'll be pressurizing that system.

You have two choices for pressurization: a water pump or an air pump.

A 12-volt RV on-demand water pump is sure nice, but costs two or three times what an air pump does. These are available from RV dealers for under $100, but you can get one from J.C. Whitney for about $60. These are part numbers 74VY8421A and 81VY2262W, the difference between them being the amount of pressure they generate and maintain. The former comes on at 20 psi and off at 35, the latter on at 13 psi and off at 18. The first draws 3 amps, and the second, 4½. These pumps are sure nice, and water pressure is available on demand, but I have my reservations about them, besides the amount of power they use.

Travel trailers aren't really designed for winter living conditions, they're mostly summer vacation shelters. Consequently, water pipes in them tend to run in odd-ball, out-of-the-way places, and during extremely cold weather (below zero) I have sometimes had them freeze in certain locations. Although I have now taken care of that by exposing lines and leaving cabinet doors open at night, I wouldn't want to take a chance on a pipe bursting — with pressurized water behind it. Pipes that are filled with water but not pressurized don't burst when they freeze — at least that's my experience, and I had them freeze a lot before I figured out what to do about it.

If you use a water pump, put a switch on it, and turn it off every night and every time you leave. You probably won't have to worry, except for the times you forget to switch it off.

What I used was an old-style 12-volt air pump I obtained cheaply. It has a rubber hose on it with an end piece that is threaded to screw onto an automotive tire valve stem, for inflating tires. My trailer was set up for such a pump in the outside storage compartment at the rear, and so I tried it. Worked fine.

I hooked it up to the batteries, with a switch in the line (on the bathroom wall), and it worked fine until the cold weather really set in. The pressure line ran under the trailer, and condensation in the line would freeze up — result: no water.

So I removed it from there, and with the help of a few pipe fittings, installed it where a plug had been in the filler line above the water tank. The air valve itself is a one-way valve, otherwise water might back up into the pump. The pump is screwed to a board that sits on the floor right next to the water tank. No freeze-ups, and all this is hidden under one of the couches.

You can buy these emergency air pumps from Kmart or just about any big department store for under $30, sometimes half that. They have 12-volt cigarette lighter plug-ins on them, but you simply cut it off and wire it. Be careful with these pumps, don't let them run too long. Some have up to 200 psi capacity, and you don't need anywhere near that much. Mine only puts out about 25 psi, and works just fine.

I used a regular house light switch for the pump, mounted on the bathroom wall within easy reach while in the shower. You always know when the pump is running, because you can hear it operating. It's impossible to walk away and forget about it. And I find that my water system loses pressure by itself after about 30 minutes, so I don't worry about bursting the pipes.

The Cistern

I first started by using 6-gallon water jugs from Wal-Mart, 2 at a time, and pouring the water directly into my trailer's water tank. But it gets to be a pain in the neck going for water every day. When I bought a third jug, that helped, and I only had to go every other day.

Figure 11
The Cistern.

But it becomes a chore to go all the time, besides the gasoline used. So I came up with an idea for a small cistern. Here's how it works:

Get 3 more plastic barrels, a 10′ section of 3″ inside-diameter PVC pipe (check your barrels first to see if this is the right size for your needs), two 45-degree elbows, a cap, and a tube of silicone. Also buy 10′ of ³⁄₈″ plastic water line, and a 12-volt submersible RV water pump. I got mine from J.C. Whitney, part number 14VY4805B. This pump is $18.95, and is only 4½″ long by 1½″ in diameter. It will fit easily through the hole in the barrel.

Dig a 6′ hole under your trailer, directly under the water tank, and put a barrel in this hole. Place it so one of the holes in the top of the drum is directly underneath where your water line will come down from the trailer.

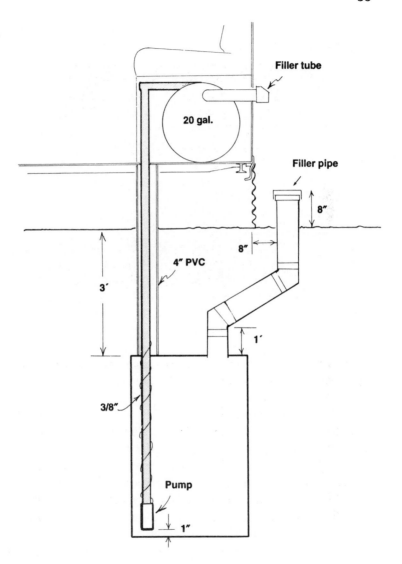

Figure 12
The Cistern.

Drill a ⅝″ or bigger hole in the trailer floor for the water line and wiring.

Pipe straight up to the hole in the floor of the trailer with the PVC. This pipe should fit directly over the flange for one of the two threaded holes in the top of the barrel. You may need to file some of the flange off with a wood rasp. Make a tight fit. Now remove the pipe.

Connect the wiring and water line to the pump, and drop it into the barrel. Make sure it's near the bottom. I held mine up about an inch, in case any sediment collects on the bottom of the barrel. Heavily silicone the flange.

Now run the water line and pump wiring through the PVC and up through the hole in the trailer floor. Silicone and install the PVC pipe into place. This is somewhat difficult, and you may find you need a small gap between the trailer and the pipe. Silicone or otherwise seal off where the pipe meets the bottom of the trailer.

Next, install the filler pipe, again using a lot of silicone. Come up with about a 1′ piece and put an elbow on it (use glue). Place the next straight section into the elbow, coming out far enough that your filler tube will be outside the trailer. Now is a good time to temporarily wire this pipe into place. Put on the next elbow, and pipe up to however high you want it. My cap is 8″ above ground.

You can now fill the cistern and backfill the barrel. The next step is to make the connection of the waterline to the trailer water tank. You'll need a valve of some kind; I used a regular household-type water valve, the kind you turn.

You'll need various fittings to accomplish this, and a small hose clamp. Use whatever works easiest and best for you. My water tank already had two plugs on it, attached to piping on the top of the tank, at the opposite end from the external filler tube. However you do it, you need the water to fill from the top of the tank, so you can hear how full it's getting, and also so you don't strain that little pump too hard.

Wire the pump to the switch, silicone around the lines coming through the floor, and *Presto!*

To fill the trailer's water tank, open the valve you installed, and remove the cap on the outside of the trailer — the water tank's filler tube. This *must* be removed during filling. It allows you to hear how full the tank is getting, but more importantly, allows the tank to fill. This little pump doesn't have the power to fill the tank without venting, which effectively pressurizes the tank. And while it's a good pump, it's not strong enough for that. You'll soon know when the tank is full, generally when it stops making noise — when you no longer hear the sound of falling water. But pay close attention when filling. Don't run the pump dry; that's bad for it.

After the tank is full, screw the cap back on outside, and close the valve. That's all there is to it. The pump is self-draining — you'll hear it when you shut it off — and so you don't have to worry about the line freezing.

Don't forget about closing the valve. If you do forget, you'll notice when you throw your pressurizing switch that it takes a long time to get water — if it comes at all. That's because you're inadvertently trying to pressurize the cistern along with the water tank.

I haul water a barrel at a time in the winter, and simply use a short garden hose to siphon the water from the barrel, as it rests in the back of my truck, down into the cistern. When it's warmer, I get two at a time. Siphon one into the cistern, and put that empty barrel on the ground. Then siphon the other barrel into the empty. When the cistern goes dry, you simply siphon your extra barrel down into it.

I do conserve water, but I'm not miserly. A cistern-full (one barrel) lasts me a whole week.

Incidentally, every once in a while you should add a few drops of chlorine to the cistern to combat any bacteria that might build up. The easiest way is to use plain old chlorine bleach, like Clorox. This is quite safe, and will not affect the drinkability of your water.

Chapter 7
Power

Some power is needed, and depending on your needs, there are several alternatives.

Power will be used for lights, the water pressure pump, communications reception (radio and TV), battery charging, and any other needs you may have, such as electric typewriters or the like.

I'm not talking about curling irons, blow-dryers, can openers, electric motors or electric heaters. A hand can opener works just fine, and the others take so much energy as not to be practical. Anything that produces heat by electricity is out of the question; so are large electric motors.

There are several sources of cheaply-obtained power, and a generator stands out foremost, at least at first. It's the cheapest and easiest to use.

Next is solar power, followed by wind generation.

There still remain several others, such as water-produced electricity, but that entails making use of that ever-elusive and very expensive stream.

Generators

Small generators are portable, easy to come by, very quiet, and only sip gasoline. I use a Honda EX650, which produces 650 watts of power. It also includes a built-in 12-volt battery charger that produces an output of 8.7 amps.

Before I had solar, I'd charge my batteries while watching the evening news on the 110-volt side of the generator.

Figure 13
Honda EX650 generator.

Figure 14
Solar panel platform.

I highly recommend purchasing one with this charging feature, since batteries will be used. You'll need it for cloudy days when your solar panels aren't charging much. Also, it can start your truck should the battery fail.

Mine runs approximately 6 hours on a half-gallon of gasoline. That's not much fuel.

But unless you watch TV all day, the generator will get most of its use when you are first setting up your homestead, powering drills and other tools. With solar, the generator is only occasionally used.

Solar Power

This is an excellent way to go, especially in areas that receive a lot of sunshine, such as where I live. There are no moving parts to wear out, and once the panels are in place, you are set. Of course, you need batteries to store the electricity produced, and an inverter to convert the power into 110 volts, but this system requires no weekly expenditure for fuel, no oil changes, and started by the sunrise, not by pulling a cord.

Solar panels produce power in 12 volts DC (direct current), and since electricity cannot be stored in 110 volts AC (alternating current), it needs to be stored in batteries.

Special batteries are made just for this purpose, but they are expensive. Some people use big old telephone-company batteries; some use golf-cart batteries; and some use regular car batteries. However, deep-cycle RV batteries work just fine, and for the amount of electricity I use, they were the best purchase. They are made for just this purpose.

You need deep-cycle batteries because you can draw them down a long way. They last longer than car batteries. They also take longer to charge, but with solar power, this is not a problem.

My solar-power setup cost a total of $545, and consists of 4 1' x 4' panels, 4 batteries, and a power inverter.

The panels cost $215 delivered, and I purchased them from Abraham Solar, Box 957, Pagosa Springs, Colorado 81147. 1-800-222-7242 or (303) 731-4675. They were used panels, but work very well, and carried a 1-year guarantee. They are rated at 17.5 volts, 87 watts, and charge at 5 amps. Mine perform better than this, due to the high altitude where I live.

These panels were a bargain, and probably won't be on the market long. The dealers purchase them from large solar projects throughout the nation that are either shutting down or replacing their panels. Keep up with listings in some of the rural/country/self-sufficiency publications.

I have four of the largest RV/Marine deep cycle batteries that Western Auto carried. They cost $260. These can also be purchased at Kmart or Wal-Mart, and many auto parts stores. Besides a regular automotive-type post terminal, RV/Marine batteries usually have an additional bolt with wing nut built in either separately next to the main post, or protruding from the top of the post itself. If it doesn't, that in itself doesn't bar its use if you're going to use metal straps for the connections. You could always drill a hole down into the post and use a short, rough-threaded screw, or make your connection at the bolt that squeezes the battery-cable end around the post.

Installation

Since direct sunlight produces the most power, some people mount their solar panels on a movable platform and simply push it to face the sun several times during the day. The east in the morning, south at noon, and towards the west in the evening. I don't need that much power, and elected to mount mine stationary, facing the south.

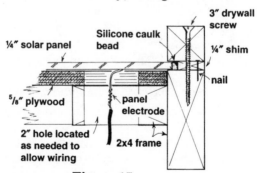

Figure 15
Solar panel installation at end of platform.

For the platform, I bought a 4'x 8' sheet of exterior grade (CDX) ⁵⁄₈″ plywood, six 2 x 4 x 8's, a large handful of 3″ drywall screws, another of 1½″ screws, 2 tubes of silicone, and a gallon of white paint, to make the platform match my trailer. This material cost $70.

I screwed 2 x 4's flat to the back of the platform, with the exception of the top one, which I glued and screwed to the trailer. With the help of my neighbor, I then hoisted the platform into position, screwed down through the plywood into that top 2 x 4, and then screwed the supporting legs to the trailer.

After adding blocks to the ends, and another 2 x 4 for a lip at the bottom (which also helps keep the platform from sagging), I laid out the platform for panels.

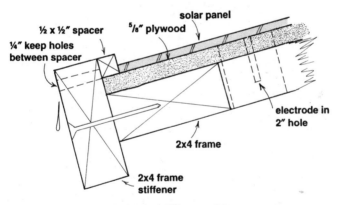

Figure 16
Solar panel installation and platform.

This platform is big enough to allow for a second set of panels, if your needs increase later. The 4 solar panels are 11 + ¾″ by 47 + ¾″ each, and so fit handily on one side of the platform.

After measuring and marking the plywood, I used a 2″-hole saw in my electric drill to cut holes for wiring. After this, I painted the entire platform with 2 coats of exterior house paint. Be sure to really cover the edges of the plywood, and the holes. Plywood is extremely vulnerable to delamination by water, so paint it well.

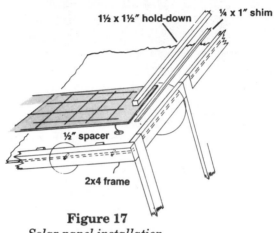

Figure 17
Solar panel installation.

Install your panels by laying them flat on the plywood, starting at the bottom. Bend the electrodes so they project through the holes you've drilled. I blocked up the panels ½" from the bottom 2 x 4 lip. Silicone all the way around the panel, and set the next panel into position. Do this with all four.

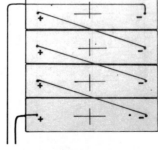

Figure 18
Solar panel wiring.

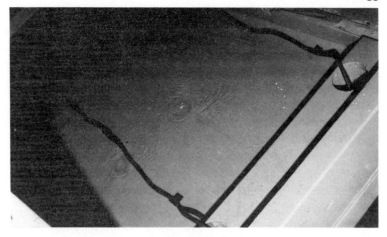

Figure 19
Underside of solar, showing wiring.

I put a ¼″ ribbing on each end, the thickness of a panel, and then installed a 2 x 2 on each end to hold the panels down. Don't tighten the screws down too hard; you don't want to break the glass. Silicone around the 2 x 2, and touch up paint.

For wiring, cut up an old extension cord.

You want to connect these panels in *series*, not parallel (see Figure 18). You'll hook up the positive of one panel to the negative of another, tying all 4 panels together.

For the wiring to your switch, use a positive from one end of the series and the negative from the other end. Run the wiring to your switch. You can use almost any kind of a switch for this; I used a regular home light switch. If the switch only accepts one of the wires, attach the switch to the positive.

From your switch, run the wiring to your batteries.

I put my batteries in the storage area off the back of my trailer. It's best to keep them fairly warm, and this does it for me. Besides, that's where the wiring for the trailer's 12-volt lighting connects.

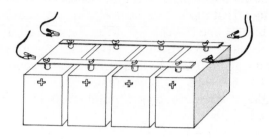

Figure 20
RV/Marine Deep Cycle Batteries in parallel.

Now, your batteries should be hooked up in *parallel*. That is, positive to positive, negative to negative. This provides 12 volts, with more amperage. You can use automotive battery cables from a department store, or metal straps.

Connect the wiring from the switch to the batteries. You can use jumper cable ends for this, also available at the department store. Also connect your trailer's 12-volt lighting.

Figure 21
Battery connections close up (at first battery).

From the batteries, run a line into a convenient place in the trailer. Install several cigarette lighter plugs from an automobile. (I use the second outlet for my cellular phone.) Get a voltmeter and install it in the line so you can monitor the condition of your batteries. I bought one at Radio Shack for $5, but you can also take one out of an automobile if it's marked with numbers. You now have 12-volt power in your trailer.

For 110 volts AC, you need a power inverter. These are available from many sources, but I got mine from the J.C. Whitney catalog. Figure up the biggest electrical load you need to run, and buy one of the appropriate size. I got the smallest "modified sine wave" inverter they had, a Stat-power PROwatt 125, part number 83XX0598T. It puts out 125 watts continuous, 200 watts for 5 minutes, and a 400 surge. It runs my 13" color TV or my word processor, no problem. This model costs $79.95, and plugs into a cigarette lighter outlet.

Presto — *power!*

Some things to remember:

Monitor your batteries. If they overcharge, turn the switch off. If you don't use a lot of power — and you leave the switch on — you could boil your batteries. No good — you'll ruin them! To be safe, throw the switch off when you leave.

Likewise, don't let your batteries get down too far. A drained battery in freezing weather will freeze at about the same temperature as water. This doesn't mean you can't use your power at night — quite to the contrary. That's what it's there for. Just don't drain them down to nothing. It's best to keep them topped off everyday. In a charged battery, the solution remains more like sulphuric acid, and won't freeze in winter. In a weak battery, the solution becomes more like water.

At night, throw your switch off. Otherwise, you'll lose just a little bit of your power by allowing the juice to flow back into the panels. If you install a diode in the line, you don't have to worry about that. Also, as an option, you can install a voltage regulator in the line from the panels to the battery, in lieu of a switch. This makes your charging completely automatic, eliminating the need for a switch. If you spend much time away, you might want to consider this. These are also available from Abraham Solar. A 15-amp regulator (enough to handle 3 sets of panels) sells for about $67.

On cloudy days, your solar panels won't put out their maximum power. At times like this, if you need to, run the generator to charge the batteries.

Keep the panels clean for optimum performance.

Chapter 8
Heat

Better figure on wood. Wood is the cheapest, most readily available way to heat a travel trailer or small mobile home.

Installing a wood stove in a travel trailer is not that hard to do — it takes about 2 days — and is the only way to heat and live cheaply at the same time. You'll back up your heat with propane, using the trailer's heater, but propane is expensive, and although you'll use some anyhow, you want to keep that to a minimum.

Stoves

My travel trailer is an 8' x 21', and my stove, which is the shape of a small barrel laid on end, is substantially larger than I need. It is 16" in diameter, and 22" in depth, excluding the handle. Somebody made it, but you would never know it. They ground the welds and painted it. I paid $80 for it at a used furniture store.

Try to get one that is as air-tight as possible. They're more efficient, meaning they leak less, and use less wood. However, don't worry too much if it's not — it doesn't take much of a fire to heat a small space such as we have.

You don't need to spend a lot of money on the wood stove. Don't buy a fancy, brand name, super-expensive model. And it doesn't need to be lined with firebrick — a coal burner. You won't burn coal, anyhow, unless you live next to a coal mine. Get one used, and don't be too concerned about looks. If you want to cook on it, get one that's set up for it.

Figure 22
*The installed stove — good ol' country
comforts in the homestead.*

Consider the best place to put it. In my case, I removed half of a built-in couch to install it. It's between the couch and the kitchen sink, right next to the hot water heater.

Consider how you're going to pipe it. What's the best way? Do you want to go through the roof? Or through a window? The wall?

In my case, I took out a window and replaced it with 2 sheets of sheet metal, one inside and one out. I had a sheet-metal shop cut this for me, but you can certainly do it yourself. I simply measured the opening and had the metal cut to fit inside the aluminum jamb, against the stops. I also had the shop cut the holes for the stove pipe in it, making them just larger than the 6″ flue.

On the floor I laid 2-inch solid cinder block, available at the lumberyard. At the back wall and the sides, I used 4-inch solid block, simply stacked up on top of each other, 4 courses high. If you want to get fancy, you can mortar the block, but I didn't.

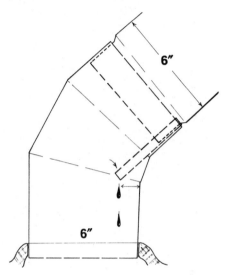

Figure 23
Drip trough at adjustable elbow.

Since my window is to the right of where the stove sits, I put a 45 degree elbow out the top of the stove, to direct the smoke towards the window. Next, I put a straight section with a damper in it, followed by a 90-degree elbow pointing at the window.

A straight section goes through the sheet metal, with small escutcheon (trim) plates on either side. Make it long enough to keep your flue 8 inches or so from the side of the trailer. Once outside, another 90 degree elbow turns upward, and 3 straight sections go up to a cap on top.

Considerations:

Put the hole for the flue in the middle of the window space. This area will get hot, and you don't want the flue too close to anything combustible.

Consider whether you want your pipes to slip over or into each other. Slipping over each other is the way it is usually done, and I did this when I first installed my stove. In other words, the upper pipe slips down over the lower pipe. However, this allows condensation and creosote to flow freely from the joints, making a mess all over the outside of your trailer, and sometimes inside.

Figure 24
Woodstove flue.

Some people reverse the pipes, as I have done. This makes any liquids flow all the way back down into the stove, not staining the side of your trailer. This is the way it is done in Europe. If you do this, make sure the 45 degree elbow out of your stove is a solid piece, not adjustable. Adjustable elbows leak stinky liquids all over your stove, and generally make a mess. If you can't find a solid one, seal the joints somehow. Another possibility is to install a piece of aluminum inside the joint where the 45 meets the straight piece. Make it long enough so the liquids drip into the stove (see Figure 23). Don't use a regular piece of metal, such as from skirting. I tried this, and it rusted out.

The flue must extend up beyond the top of your trailer. Tall flues work better, and you don't want any sparks falling onto your roof.

An installation like this is generally self-supporting, but you will need to strap the flue to the trailer, because of wind. Use wire, metal strapping, or whatever's handy, but tie it down.

Clean the flue frequently. I do mine every 3 months, whether it needs it or not. Take it off in sections and run a stick through it.

The Propane Heater

All travel trailers of this size have them. The older ones, like mine, amount to a space heater enclosed in a grill. Mine has a Coleman wall heater built in near the door, with a thermostat near the center of the trailer. Newer ones are required by law to be forced-air, meaning they have a blower attached. If yours does, you'll have to power the blower with your batteries. I prefer the old kind. But whatever kind you have, the unit must be functional.

Frequently, older heaters like this leak fumes. Mine did, too. But you can fix this with a product called "Furnace Cement," available in a hardware store. It comes in small tubs the size of a coffee cup, and costs about $2. There're two kinds: gray and black. The gray is more like mortar, and the black is more gooey. I prefer the black; it's easier to use, and holds better. Go over the seams generously, and also where the vent comes out. Let this cement dry for a day, and you should be in good shape.

Consider getting a propane tank from your local gas company. Changing little bottles all the time gets to be a chore. In winter, I found I had to fill one every 4 days, so I rented a 250 gallon tank from our local co-op. It costs $4 a month.

The total cost for delivery, gas line to the trailer, hookup, and 100 gallons of fuel was $241.

Wood

Not much needs to be said here. Dry wood burns better than wet, and wood dries by being cut, split, stacked and aged. Do it.

Hard woods burn better than soft; that is, they last longer and burn hotter. However, soft woods are easier to cut and split, and generally season faster.

How to tell soft woods from hard: needles or leaves. Soft woods, like pine, spruce, and fir have needles. Hard woods — oak, maple, etc. have leaves.

There are exceptions. Piñon, which has needles, is very hard — hard to cut and split, and long to dry. But it burns long and hot.

Aspen, which has leaves, is fairly soft. It's easy to split and dries quickly. But it also burns quickly.

I burn a mixture of aspen and piñon. The aspen, I light fires with and make a bed of coals. The piñon I add after it's going, and it lasts a long time, especially at night. Bank a fire with piñon and it lasts a long, long time.

A few words on chain saws: you get what you pay for. Depends on your financial condition. You can spend $500 on a Stihl that will last a decade or longer, or you can buy an Eager Beaver on sale new for $100 that will last for several years.

I go with the Beaver. It's a very reliable saw, but wears out with hard work. It's kind of like a disposable saw, but if you treat it well, keep it sharp, and don't cut firewood for a living, it should last you at least several years. Watch for them on sale at department stores.

Splitting. Good exercise with a sledge hammer and a wedge. I enjoy it.

Fires

I use kerosene to start cold fires. Just throw a few pieces of wood in the stove and squirt a little kerosene on it. A plastic dish soap or syrup bottle works well for this. Kerosene won't explode when you light it, instead flaring up slowly. It doesn't take much; you'll soon find out how much to use.

A word of caution: light only cold fires with this. If there's any red coals at all, it's best to just stir up the fire and leave the door open till it catches. Kerosene squirted on red coals will start vaporizing, and will *foomp!* when lit.

Some people use diesel fuel, and it acts about the same way. I use kerosene because I have it on hand anyway for my kerosene lamp.

Incidentally, I don't use a grate in my wood stove. When you burn wood constantly, you have to empty the ashes weekly. The grate is just a pain in the neck at such times, and keeping logs on the coals is one way to keep them burning, especially if they're not completely dried yet. Just stir the fire up occasionally, and everything will burn completely.

You'll soon find that a fire uses up all the fresh air in a trailer. Just crack a window open. Sometimes, if it's real windy, you'll find that you may get smoke coming out of the stove. Open a window upstream, close the others, and that usually takes care of it. For this reason, I don't recommend putting plastic over the windows of the trailer.

The wind can be very fickle, and on different days you'll have different windows open. I also don't recommend covering the vent in the top of the trailer. It's easy to build a fire that is too hot, and opening the vent is the quickest way to dump the hot air.

At night, or anytime you are leaving the trailer for hours at a time, turn down the stove by closing the air vents nearly all the way, and closing the flue damper most of the way. You'll notice that this immediately makes the wood stove hotter, but this is because the heat is no longer going out the flue, and is effectively bottled up in the stove. However, this is short lived, and the fire goes down because of lack of air to burn, because you have closed the air vents. Because of closing the damper, most of the smoke remains within the stove, and smoke doesn't contain much oxygen.

Chapter 9
Refrigeration

Propane. A trailer of this size generally has a small propane refrigerator installed in it as factory equipment. Many, however, no longer work. That is not a problem, and I'll go into that below.

Figure 25
Good ol' country comforts in your travel-trailer home!

The propane fridge in mine had been removed and replaced with an apartment-sized electric unit. Naturally, my small generator wouldn't push that, and in any case, it wouldn't work because I'd have had to run the generator around the clock. A generator that never stops, will, sooner or later. I'm talking about wearing it out.

So when I first came out here, I installed an icebox. It was fall, and as the cold weather progressed, I was soon able to make my own ice by setting a tray of water outside, overnight. This worked well, but still left no freezer capacity, with the exception of a cooler placed in the shade on the north side of my trailer. The cooler worked just fine in freezing temperatures, of course, but as soon as it started to warm up, spoiled food.

After talking with my neighbor, who uses 2 full-sized propane refrigerators in his mobile home, I obtained a small propane unit from another trailer. The man had tried it, and it didn't work.

People commonly believe that these use a lot of gas, but a propane refrigerator of this size actually costs less money to operate in warm weather than the expense of buying block ice every other day, and provides you with a small freezer in the bargain.

Figure 26
Don't leave that refrigerator door open!

Aside from the coolant itself, there are no moving parts, and a propane fridge uses only a small pilot light type of flame for operation. The unit must be vented outside, of course, but trailers of this size are generally already set up for this.

These units operate on a liquid-to-gas and gas-back-to-liquid basis, the gas flame (heat) providing the means of transfer. The liquid refrigerant is turned into gas by the heat. It rises in the piping. As it rises, it cools. As it then cools back into a liquid, it produces a cold temperature, which directly cools the food compartment.

What generally goes wrong with these boxes are two things: either the refrigerant leaks out, which is unlikely, or the refrigerant settles from lack of use and doesn't perform adequately.

If it's leaked out, you can have them recharged by an appliance repairman. However, this is usually not the case, and the next method of making them operable should be tried — first.

Remove the unit from the trailer, completely. Clean all gas lines out, including the filter (looks like a small automotive gas line filter). Then clean out the orifices in the gas burner with a small needle, pin, or something of that sort, being careful not to enlarge the holes (propane consumption would increase, and your fridge may over-perform, meaning you may not be able to keep the entire food compartment from freezing).

Next put the unit upside-down in the back of your truck, and leave it there (with all gas lines or orifices taped over) for several days, and go about your business. Just being turned on its head for several days is usually enough to stir up the refrigerant. However, I drove around with it in the back of my truck for three days, as I conducted my day-to-day affairs, believing this would *really* help stir it up.

After several days, re-install it, checking the gas line connections for leaks. Then light the flame, and give it 24 hours to cool enough for use. This usually does it. If it doesn't, your refrigerant is probably gone.

Another possibility might be that the two-stage pilot light is malfunctioning for some reason. Check to be sure it works in two stages, by turning the temperature control from defrost to operation. The flame should rise when the knob is turned, but the rise is very small indeed, and you have to pay attention to catch it. These things don't use much gas.

By stirring up the contents thus, you should have a fully functional refrigerator with freezer. These actually work very well indeed.

An interesting note: the area I live in is windy at times, and I found that a strong, sustained wind affected the operation of my fridge — it started defrosting because the wind was blowing the heat of the flame away. I closed up one side of the vent on top of the trailer — the side facing the prevailing wind — and partially covered the air intake on the side of the trailer. That took care of the problem.

Closing Statement

I hope you enjoyed this book, and are full of ideas about how to prepare for homesteading.

If you don't already have a truck, you should get one, preferably a four-wheel drive. Gather all your tools beforehand — look for bargains and visit garage sales for things you'll need.

Try to get all your bills paid off, and stash something away you can live on while you're setting up your homestead. If you have money to live off of, you can concentrate on getting your home set up, without the additional pressure of looking for a job — or giving all your time to it — and then trying to work around your home in your spare time. In my case, it took me a little while, but I saved until I had a year's worth of expenses in the bank. Let me tell you, it's a wonderful feeling to be set up on your own property, and not owe anybody *anything*.

I hope you do well on your new homestead, and the best of luck to you.

Index

YOU WILL ALSO WANT TO READ:

THE BEST BOOK CATALOG IN THE WORLD!!!

We offer hard-to-find books on the world's most unusual subjects. Here are a few of the topics covered IN DEPTH in our exciting new catalog:

- *Hiding/Concealment of physical objects! A complete section of the best books ever written on hiding things.*
- *Fake ID/Alternate Identities! The most comprehensive selection of books on this little-known subject ever offered for sale! You have to see it to believe it!*
- *Investigative/Undercover methods and techniques! Professional secrets known only to a few, now revealed to you to use! Actual police manuals on shadowing and surveillance!*
- *And much, much more, including Locks and Lockpicking, Self-Defense, Intelligence Increase, Life Extension, Money-Making Opportunities, Human Oddities, Exotic Weapons, Sex, Drugs, Anarchism, and more!*

Our book catalog is 292 pages, 8½ x 11, packed with over 800 of the most controversial and unusual books ever printed! You can order every book listed! Periodic supplements keep you posted on the LATEST titles available!!! Our catalog is $5.00, including shipping and handling.

Our book catalog is truly THE BEST BOOK CATALOG IN THE WORLD! Order yours today. You will be very pleased, we know.

LOOMPANICS UNLIMITED
PO BOX 1197
PORT TOWNSEND, WA 98368

Name_____

Address_____

City/State/Zip_____

Now accepting Visa and MasterCard. For credit card orders *only*,
call 1-800-380-2230. 9am to 4pm, PST, Monday thru Friday.